the stars in her crown

I'm so sorry
I'm sorry you will know this world through the windows of a broken home
I did everything I could to keep us together
I'm sorry you won't witness mutual love between the two souls responsible for your existence
I'm sorry I didn't recognize the boy behind the mask of a man before I gave him pieces of my heart so willingly, so unhesitant
Some people don't show who they really are until hardships arise, and I saw potential when I looked into his eyes
But I wish I knew, oh how I wish I knew
I'm sorry that you may feel tugged in different directions on special days
I'll do my best to make things normal for you
I'm sorry I was so venturesome, so wanting of love, that I latched on to someone who wasn't sent for me
I'm sorry I couldn't give you what you deserve
I wanted you to experience a home with two loving parents
One that I imagined
I wanted to be the example of true love for you
To teach you what I've learned about being a wife and mother
I wanted to be able to give you a stable home, so that you wouldn't have to pack your bags every other weekend
I wanted you to be closer to your father than I was with mine, to be able to spend every day creating memories
I didn't want you to have to look forward to his turn
I'm sorry I couldn't give you better
But I couldn't be selfish and give you nothing
I pray you learn from me, and I pray my story has an ending you will look up to

I dedicate these collections of poems to you, to teach you of your magic and your worth. I hope my stories will help you make better decisions than I did. I know you will have your own experiences in this life, as your mommy I'm here equip you for them.

I love you with my soul, forever.

Love

Wanderer

Home

Woman

Love

six signs ignored because I loved you

One. You keep count of mistakes while still expecting yours to be forgotten. You have lukewarm traits and conditional affection, instant erection to anyone of the opposite sex and, I'm tired. I'm starting to think you're not only blind with your eyes but with your heart too, because you think so highly of yourself but refuse to look beneath the surface. You take the days for granted, content with only checking on your loved ones twice a month or when it's brought to your attention that you've been distant. Asking how are you, expecting the answer to be "good" but when it's not you don't know how to be there, an ear, a listener, a shoulder. Yet, you wonder why you felt like you're always the last to know. You're not, you just didn't care to listen the first time.

Two. You lie and you actually believe them. Your words spill too quickly from your mouth that you get caught up a week later. How easily you use your words with no regard for how your lies will affect others.

Three. You get high off of my lows. My pain brings you much joy. With you, nothing feels certain. Nothing feels like a step forward, nothing feels like it's being fixed. It's just a constant maybe.

Four. You lack the basic knowledge of compassion and respect. For someone who's big on having loyal people in his life you're very unreliable, very dismissive, very emotionally unavailable. How quickly you're able to cut people off for things you won't tolerate, but expect to be forgiven for your short comings time and time again. Selfish.

Five. You should've never had me to begin with.

Six. For some reason, you think I need you. And it's actually quite funny that you think you acquire anything I'm in need of. I've asked you for kind words in my ear when my when my insecurities scream inside my body and that bothers you. You think I need you. Encouragement and validation are two different things, I wish you understood the difference. You see I don't need you to tell me who I am, I'm saying I may need a lift when I've my lows get heavy. I don't need you to tell me I'm a good mother, I know that, but there are times when I don't feel like the best Mother at that given moment. I don't define myself by what you think of me, but a little nudge of encouragement goes a long way. See there are times when I doubt myself or start to drag a little bit, but I still know I am. At that time when you see me begin to droop, a little ounce of encouragement could've made a difference. But because I pick myself up out of quicksand... not you or nobody hold the power to sink me and I don't need you to catch me.

tell me what's on your mind
I'm curious to know if there's anything I can help you with
if there's anything that needs a little bit of nurturing
how can I be of service
point out your insecurities to me
so I can kiss them delicately
grab hold of my hand I want to show you what I see
did you know gold oozes from beneath your feet when you walk
so gracefully
how come you don't see how you bring laughter
inside the lives of the people who embrace you
let me show you how much I adore you
how I'd love to explore you
cum for you and come before you
to give you a love I know no one has ever shown you
can I do that for you?
see I know what you deserve, and I know that I can give it
if you let me, I can love you in ways you never thought could be given
tell you I love you in more ways than just verbal
I'm going to show you
every negative thought you have
I'm gonna love it out of you.
I'd love to create a mini you
and I would only hope he'll possess every trait of you

you are my poppy flower in heat
my sunflower in weeds
you're my springtime
fresh smelling mint and thyme
you're my lemonade in mid-day
you're my summer
the melody of my song
the sunset in my eyes
you're my blue sky
you're my vacation and my home
my voice of reason
the strength in my bones
my calm and my storm
you're my frankincense resin
you're the tingles on my skin
you're energy pure and strong
like a new moon
you're my sunshine in the afternoon

hands caressing my natural curves
our blended scent fills every corner of the room
my garden is no longer guarded
I can't keep from sprouting seeds, my flower creates nectar for you
you expose my neck by pushing your jaw up against mine, outlining the curve of my arch with your fingertips, chills rush down as you make your way through me
oh how she smiles for you, how after years of harvesting she blossomed for you
patiently you watered her for months upon months, and for that she's grateful of you
lift up for a second, I'd like to see you, watch you as I let you into my garden
keep tending to me lovingly
keep nurturing this flower I've held for keepsake
I want to make you the permanent keeper
I look at you and my world is calm
every problem floating around me falls beneath the ground at the presence of you
I can't be anything but amazed when I'm with you
in you I've found hope again
I see the good in people again, I give chances again, I lie above you in awe
brushing my hands over the invisible scars above your heart that are strength in my eyes
I know how to hide my feelings just as good as you
keeping the pain of the near absence of you silent
I'm hurting myself, but I can't release you
I mean I can but then I'll miss you
like a sleeping baby that no longer feels the presence of her mother
I'll cry out for you in my dreams
I'm not ready for this scene in my life to end
Though I know what's right and what's best

I'll keep loving you in silence instead
and keep hope that our next chapter
will start with "*I thee wed*"

what are you afraid of he said
what exactly is your motive I said
help me, help you
find the missing pieces or replace them
I want to know what you plan to do
now that you've unfolded me
do you plan to cherish me and hold onto me
or was your mission just to open me
why are you so dedicated to knowing my story
to use it against me
or to understand me
trust me he said
let me love you he said
I do trust you I said
and that's why I'm afraid
I've trusted before
and I wish I hadn't

I've painted pictures in my dreams of you or someone familiar
you've shown me light in the midnight forests
I have no doubts you're in my corner
I want to savor this story
we've written poems with our sweat
if ever you forget my eyes when yours and mine met
I hope you remember how they dilated at the sight of your presence
allured, I wanted to be yours
a beautiful being, one I've painted in my dreams before
just stay a little longer, I feel like I've been needing something like you
I feel like you've been searching for something in me
something only someone like me can give to you
tell me you need me like I need you
I can feel pieces of me begin to fall like the leaves in autumn
as the days lessen, our time together has been decreasing
collecting as many memories before the end of our season
because the day I can no longer hold your hand, will be the day I will no longer know how to withstand
separation has knocked on my door before I'm not new to this, I'm just still not used to it so, before our time makes its end
just kiss me a little softer until then
hold me a little tighter
make love to me a little longer
just, stay a little longer

I realize I may never be yours to have
your heart may never notice me
we've experienced similar aches and pains
but yours are much more healed than mine
you guard it with heavy metals
you hide it with opaque shades
but can't you see I'm not like them
I don't share their ways
don't place doubt on me without being given the
opportunity to prove
it amazes me that I still attempt to mend
a broken heart by offering
the crumbs left of mine
this heart has been beaten by heavy weights
but still beats a loving rhythm
still finds the time to care even for those who don't care to look into it
because who knows if they might need it
this heart of mine still loves

blank stares and trembling from the inside out
silently praying for a sprinkle of goodness over my life
thoughts scattered trying to find peace of mind
or the piece of my mind that can piece together whatever I've been needing
at a time where all I've been chasing is something
comfortable, unwavering
I can't seem to keep my mind from wandering
wondering why I'm too much to handle or too good but not good enough to get ready for
jumping from topic to topic, moods fluctuating
inconsistent, uncontrollable
I've lost battles against my conscience
too tired to pick my own brain
I've gone insane over time
not literally but I think it's weird how my tears
form then disappear never fully leaving the ducts
relentlessly giving up pieces of me to people I thought I could trust
I expected people to treasure me
self-willed, I can't let them see me at my lowest
too guarded to fall, too cautious to be called victim
too weary to keep giving
now I don't give too much these days, because I know they don't cherish much these days
they don't value love these days and I'm too valuable to settle for less
so, I've mastered the art of fake smiling, they never see me at my lowest
or because of my smile they never seem to notice
that I've never truly felt I was enough
much like the cancer crab in me these shells house secrets unimaginable
these walls were built to keep me safe
away from the things that throw off my chakras, not to mention throw off my hormones, I'm fixated on getting to know me

my apologies, I think I'm too used to being forgotten
I lost myself searching for something to fulfil the empty spaces
I think I lost myself searching for those who walked away
I hear my conscience flow through the wind
I don't wish to pretend anymore

friendly visits both enjoying the company
both working on each other not realizing it
but fixing each other
best friends by day, effortless laughs
too afraid to admit this is something more
lovers when the night ends
jealous when your time is spent
keeping someone else company
do you still want me in your right mind
liquid brings out the courage to express
hidden feelings
then come morning we often forget
what was said but I remembered
you kissed my cheek lightly
I'm your baby when intoxicated
sedated
when you're asleep I watch over you in
admiration

I've stretched my arms to capacity, fall into me
I have ears that latch on to the slightest bit of sadness
eyes that detect unfamiliar patterns
I've watched your smile go from blinding to dim
I stopped gazing at the sun because your smile is more radiant
I've prayed for you since dawn, I asked the winds to bring you the
peace you've longed
the mental strength you desire
I've sung hymns under my breath to the sky
to bring rain that washes away every weight you bear
to cleanse the unwanted
silence and solitude are needed for the mind
listen to the inner thoughts you have mastered the art of ignoring

I keep you tucked in my memories
never wanted to forget you
I keep you folded in my pocket
never wanted to lose you
I keep you in my peripheral
never wanted to lose sight of you
I keep you in my palm
never wanted to let go
I keep you in my heart
never wanted to love again
but yet, I still did

temporary forever's and short-lived happiness
I'm starting to believe I'll never have this dream I've planted inside of me
I'm starting to think there's no such thing of having something
I can call mine

she loves in silence.
she ignores the burn in her palms that yearns for his touch.
she's ignoring the loudness of her love waiting to gracefully spill on him.
she loves in silence.
because love has never been her friend.
silence is her only protection against another love lost, another permanent scar.
she's tired. too scared to allow access.
but she's a natural nurturer so sometimes she has to catch herself.
she touches him softly, leans on him for strength, she looks into his eyes and can see him for who he is.
she sees him vulnerable and compassionate, yet she overlooked his armor and defense mechanisms.
she ignores the chills she gets from his touch, the constant need to fill the void of missing him.
rapid increasing speed of her heartbeat as he caresses her skin delicately.
because she knows love has always left her, she fights back tears, knowing she'll never have him, in the ways she yearns for.
her throat tightens as she locked into his grip, arms with the feeling of security wrapped around her, she loses the battle with her emotions and lets her tears fall silently, indulging in the feeling she can only wish will last a lifetime.
she loves, silently and wildly.

you are the company I never want to leave
you are the water I needed to grow through concrete
the voice I needed to hear when I thought about letting myself go
you knew that's not what I meant when I asked you to set me free
I've often felt your hand holding my right palm
the answers to my fears in psalm

we often look to others to evaluate us on our importance

to assure us of our own beautiful attributes

when did our ability to see beauty in ourselves before less of value

reassurance is something only the insecure need

God already placed on our shoulders a blanket of security

and yet we still want for the approval of humanity

when did we start to lose trust in ourselves

when did we lose us

when did we start overextending ourselves to prove our worthiness

when did our worth become measured by material things and society

there is still hope for mankind

let's take a step back, let's rewind

are you even real?
I poke you in your sleep just to make sure
and pray over you to keep you pure
after all these years of friendship
I never noticed the man that I pictured in my mind
was always in front of me
he's so refreshing and calming
like the smell on pumpkin in early autumn
oh the joy of knowing a new season is approaching
and in this new season, I am a new woman
the time I took for myself was worth it
as I stepped out of solitude there you were
with your hand reaching out for mine
patient and reassuring
you waited, you insisted, you were persistent
consistently showing your heart to me
are you even real?
teaching me daily about myself
helping me evolve and grow
supporting my goals and helping that I bring them into fruition
reassuring me in my mothering skills
stepping up as a figure to my greatest blessing with no hesitation
he is my safe home, he is my church, he is my childish bone
he is my teacher, he is also my student
he reciprocates, he expresses and listens
he is it
for me

Wanderer

what kind of writer are you?

I write because my voice is often neglected
because I was cursed with a height that is often overlooked
I write because people don't respect a calm tone during an argument,
and I don't have the energy to raise mine
I write when I need understanding of my own thoughts
and when opinions outside of me become too demanding
I write to unravel the knots and tangles of a million thoughts and
questions
so I can get to the roots of my depression
I write to tame the fire on my tongue that has enough secrets to burn
you to ashes
so I'll spare you sis
I write because I spilled my heart from my mouth before, and he gave me
his ass to kiss
so since then, I write because I'm a bit of a pacifist
I contain this beast with each stroke of this pen
I write because it's hard to give in
to trust once more, to love once more
when you've already given everything
I write to understand myself more

I don't understand the ways of the world
I get frustrated with the mentalities of others
I've always had a wild imagination
I've always seen things abstractly, subconsciously looking
beyond the surface of people, of nature, of words, etc.
when you see things differently than the people around
you, you never feel like you have anybody
I've always mentally felt alone
but the rise and fall of the sun
vibrant flowers and trees
calming winds and soothing rain
help me to remember there's beauty in this world

I'm sorry Lord, I was not patient
I created this mess on my own, and it's getting harder to clean up
I don't believe in erasing, I believe in embracing so I've decided to stick with this
Feelings started to form way before the news, so I feel like I want to keep it
He and I both have some work to do
What better way to do that than by each other's side
But lately the other side has gotten cold
Things haven't been smooth as shaved wood but I'm the only one willing to bend
I'm the only one extending hands beaten and scarred from previous situations but still, willing to extend
Still willingly to hold on
This tiny heartbeat needs me, I didn't dream of going through this alone
But I must remember your presence is wanted but not needed
If you don't want to be around, then don't be
I just thought you would want to be the difference
Instead you're okay with the distance and the tears you seem to bring out of me almost, instantly
I'm not forcing you, I just hope you want to be a better father than the one given to you
I hope history doesn't repeat

I was once a bright star in the night sky
And I was once a piece of broken glass
I have thought of myself highly
And I have criticized my every move
I have been carefree
Then I started being careful
When opinions started to matter to me
No matter what state I'm in
No matter what chapter of my life
Opinions will always be there
So I live for me

I stopped opening up, as a form of protecting my heart
being quiet soon turned into antisocial after continuously being
torn down, taken for granted and abandoned.
In my logic, my voice, my words, and my love made people afraid
of me.
Which in turn made it hard for me to express myself because in my
head I'm thinking I shouldn't say this, they may not understand it,
or it may not come out right etc.
so most times, I say nothing.
I thought I had rebuilt myself from the ground up, but it turns out I
just put wallpaper over chipped paint. I still have the same wounds.
They're much smaller but still there. I cry at the fact that I'm
overflowing with love to the top of my head, and it's just settled
there, suffocating me. I have it here, for all to see but afraid to give
it because every time I spill a little bit onto something I feel is
deserving, it ends up being a waste.

depression has been a part of my life
sometimes it's cause and effect
sometimes there's no source, just a feeling
sometimes I can explain the way I feel, sometimes I can't
I can try to pick my brain, try to piece things together
try to uplift myself, try to find peace
but I never find it
sometimes I hide behind myself
welcoming everyone with open arms
I used to give hugs a lot
people use to think I was just a hugger
but really, I just needed comfort
from anyone

chills jostle at my skin
a wave of sensation dances through my bones
summer
I've imagined bumblebees, iced sweet tea and scones
early morning, hummingbirds poking at the center of misty flowers
If I didn't have responsibilities I could sit and stare at what's around me for hours
watch your surroundings my mother always hounded
embrace what's around you
I used to have a habit of counting
the yellow lines on the street
the squares in the tile floor
how many seconds it took to empty the air from my core
observant

I am the queen of the trees, my thoughts whistle in the wind
Who knows what it feels like to be incomplete
Constantly looking for the pieces you've lost along the way, or the pieces that were stolen or left behind purposely
I've been searching for something but unsure of what or who or if it even is
I've asked around, I've prayed and prayed, I've tried to remember or I've yet to believe
Who knows what it feels like when you don't know what's missing
I wish I was the water you needed to flourish
I wish I was the light you needed in order to see
I wish you would have known my worth the day you met me

when I see people like me

enjoying life, creating life, breathing love into their veins. all I can feel is pain. I don't have enough words for poetry anymore, my time is spent thinking, my mind full of confusion. trying to understand my own feelings. I sit on the panel of my window. legs folded, my chin rests on my weary bones. time goes unnoticed, formulating odes to get me through the lows. wondering what it feels like to be home. days pass wishing I could feel a pinch of something majestic. wishing I could relive a glimpse of my childhood when everything wasn't so difficult to understand. it just made sense, or these thoughts just didn't exist. I don't carry a home inside of me but my blood sprouts across the south. I'm a southern belle. I have memories that spread six hundred miles, friends still connected despite the annoyance of distance. I cut off pieces of me at each rest stop my parents told me was home. what's it like to grow up without the fear goodbye. what's it like to be able to come back to what you've always known. to see marks in the walls that represent your growth. to sit in the chair your mother used to rock you to sleep. what's it like to have a home with roots deep underneath.

this morning
I let my hair fall out of the bun I sleep in
I pushed some stray ends behind my ears out of my face to see the aftermath of crying myself to sleep
too tired to do anything to myself I left the house as is
some carryout food still on the counter
herbal tea still brewing
soft voices still coming from my television
my bedroom window cracked just enough to make my curtain ripple
roaming into a forest but I can't feel
I'm running but I can't feel the ground
I look down to see my bare feet sprinting as if I had a destination
as if something or someone was waiting for me
as if the purpose of this trek, was me running from something
I can hear the wind passing my ears quickly
Birds singing their morning song, the sun just barely peeking through the trees
I think I'm running towards the rays
I think I'm searching for the light in my world
For nirvana
I think the answers to my questions are nonexistent
I run in my dreams because while awake
I want to run away from the world

I'm sorry I forgot to smile while I was hurting
But smiling really isn't the go-to when I'm mourning
I forgot that I'm still beautiful in the morning
Even with bags below my eyes from drowning my pillow in sadness
I forgot to stop blaming myself
There's nothing more I could have done
To keep them from hurting me
I forgot that I wasn't supposed to fall anymore
I forgot that I was focusing on myself more
I think the light in you was too blinding
I forgot to stop asking to be saved
I remembered I shouldn't have to
I've prayed for the day I can be at peace
In hopes to find someone who could see
That I'm worthy
More than just a pretty smile
More than a cute and quiet underlying of a mystery
More than just something to do
More than just someone to use
I've prayed myself to sleep with tears falling
At the bridge of my nose
Asking for these scars to heal a little faster
For this needle and thread to be a little stronger
Cause somehow these wounds like to be exposed
These scars will never let me be
But maybe, these scars are what makes me, me
I used to think someone will see them and want to save me
I keep waiting for someone to see the light in me
Or to breathe life back into me
I keep waiting for the day I can stop being afraid of me
I forgot to stop crawling into that hole when life begins to be too much
When the answer is too complicated to find
When the truth is too painful to face

You were busy searching for flaws in me
While I was overlooking yours

I’ve been here before, I know it
I’ve met you somewhere or been around you
I’ve fell for you before
It feels like I already know what your kisses taste like
Like I already know the words you're going to say to lure me in
Like I’ve already loved you before
I think I’ve fucked on you before
Like I already know how the story begins and ends
It always ends, with you
Like I already know how bittersweet your love is
Like I already felt the feeling of missing you
Hurting for you

don’t come find me
maybe two years earlier and three heartbreaks ago I would’ve liked to be found
cause sometimes I do get lonely but not today
I want to stay lost right now, for a while, safely in hiding, safely in my haven.
I don't need no one to confide in
that’s where I messed up the last time
I'm okay where I am, just leave me to wander
I don't plan on letting anyone in
love always felt like winter
beautiful but cold

Color me vibrant. Draw me with the smile I've been trying to find again.
Color me in yellow and orange, help me balance my navel chakra.
Reveal my true colors, hello black Mona Lisa.
I just want to be your muse. Use me as an aspiration, paint me pretty.
Paint me raw, uncut, natural. Paint, me.
Color my eyes brown as the soil used to bury my burdens.

Color me cold. Shut down, shut out, and closed in. Color me scared.
Color my shape, round brown and sassy.
Pinky up cause I'm something like ghetto classy. Color me passive. Draw my feet tired from walking in circles, cycling around familiar people I've never met before.
Draw me alone, and forgotten. Draw my heart rotten.

my prayers will never go unanswered
I've seen the works of God
after death was at my front door
one too many times
I've seen sickness fade overnight
and financial burdens lifted
I've seen prayers answered through signs and word of mouth
I've seen scars healed after continuously sitting in solitude,
fasting in prayer, yearning for change, eager for happiness
I've been damaged by abandonment and society
I've seen my way through the deepest pits of depression
hello
father or mother or entity, forgive me if I've labeled you incorrectly
forgive me for the questions I have about you
I only want to know you better
to walk around heaven together
to love you forever
I only want you to keep me sane until then
I didn't know of salvation until I let you in
you found me, and everyday I'm grateful
for your mercy

as beneficial as it is, I get tired of rebuilding myself
my granny always says smile, you're too pretty to be frowning
you're too brown to not look approachable
ain't nobody gon' want you 'less you seem approachable
so smile
if you want someone to notice you
I'm starting to think my smile brings the wrong people in
catches the eyes of tainted souls
brings forth the wrong attention, I've noticed
my smile is very welcoming, but my frown shielded me from my enemies
protected me from many things but also caused the ones I wanted to
overlook me
despite how crooked it is, I think my smile is contagious
cause everyone expects to see it
like it's a part of me, like it's what makes other people happy
but what about the days when I'm not
I feel like I've been everyone else's light
giving pieces of me that I need for myself
I've only ever wanted someone to look at me and think I'm worth everything
I don't have another restart in me
So no, I don't want to be approachable
I hope I scare off everyone who tries to get close enough
to hurt me any more than what's already done
you won't see this smile for a while
you won't hear this laugh come around
you won't see these eyes light up
at least not until I feel safe again
at least not until I'm comfortable enough in my skin
to know I'm too bulletproof to be broken

to my father, I'm sorry if I disappointed you
If I put time into certain men, you didn't approve
I guess I deserve everything I've been through
to my brothers, every day I need your protection
I'm sorry if I ever told you I can handle myself
If I had let you
maybe you could have helped me walk away
before I was left
before I was touched
before I was hurt
before everything
about me changed

Home

Week 5

September 12th 2018

I am a home

Twenty-three, single and expecting

It's crazy that I've still never been in a *real* relationship

One worth remembering
One worth teaching you about without embarrassment of my weaknesses
Still haven't experienced what it is to be loved, whole
Still haven't found someone who considers my happiness
And I still don't understand this life
I don't know if I can give you the right answers, but I can give you advice
I'm still very much afraid with not one clue on how to do this right

But I will, do this right or to the best of my ability and then some

I promise, you'll be alright, *we* will be alright

Week 7

Mommy is tired. And depressed. Daddy isn't much help these days not that he ever was even before we conceived. Mommy feels very alone and scared in this country with no family, no friends. And I just wish I was home surrounded by family and friends. Being in the service is stressful enough, but being in the service and pregnant, whoo! That's something. So far, I've only cried once, I haven't thrown up in 3 days, I'm craving cheese enchiladas and my patience is a ticking time bomb.

Week 8

Mommy has reached a new stage of depression. I'm ashamed of myself that I considered ending this. I'm ashamed of how weak I've become. How I let this energy weigh me down and defeat me. I have cried myself to sleep while holding you. I have watched your father laugh from a distance, ignoring the image of me in his peripheral.

Letting me walk alone, carrying loads both seen and unseen. This isn't how I pictured having you. So far, I've been doing this alone and it's breaking me.

Week 19

Mommy has had a hard time finding the desire to write. A hard time finding the strength to talk about what I feel. I still feel very much alone, even though I can feel the presence of you now. I'm still scared and stuck. At week 16 we found out that you are a girl. I was so happy, but your father ruined that moment. He is still distant, still closed off. Some days he tries, some days he couldn't care less about my well-being. The other day he let me walk to the store in 20 F° degree weather while he sat in a heated car. My back gives me the most pain, I often feel tense in my upper back, shoulders, and neck. Sometimes I ask him to rub it, he doesn't. I just need comfort, I need someone by my side, someone that takes care of me because they understand what I'm going through. He doesn't, he doesn't understand moreover he doesn't care. He'd rather someone else, anyone else do those things for me that he's too lazy to do. I'm grateful for the people in my company, some of them really look out for me. They make sure I'm okay, and ask me if I need anything. I am grateful and appreciative of them. My girlfriend bought me a whole pack of waters that I didn't ask for, but I guess she's heard me complain about being dehydrated and not being able to carry a pack of waters up 8 floors. I was truly grateful. In the back of my mind I just wish the father of my child took care of me like that.

Week 20

I feel like you've been up for 2 days. You didn't let me sleep last night, you were moving all night. Now it's 10am the next morning and you're still moving. But whenever I try to record you moving you stop. You must be shy and timid like me. Mommy doesn't want you to be timid. I'll teach you what I've learned about owning all that is you, confidently.

Week 24

Happy 6 months. Mommy feels you every day and I can see my tummy move when you kick or whatever you do in there.

I'm finally preparing to go home to have you. Mommy is making sure we share the same birthplace. I'm a little sad to be leaving your father, he doesn't know how much I care for him despite everything he's put me through. He is a lot of the reason why I've been so sad, and I feel like only he can fix that pain but he's not willing to. I know that this is just a phase he's going through, and I'm praying and believing that it will pass. I'm praying that he will realize what's in front of him. You.

Week 30

Mommy's having trouble breathing, walking, standing, getting up after sitting, sitting up after lying down. My face is so swollen it looks like I had an allergic reaction to something. I can feel your arms and your feet when you move around. You kick so hard that I can actually poke you. I think you like when I poke you because you always hit me back. You're getting so heavy, causing me to be more and more tired but luckily my supervisors are caring so they don't ask too much of me. I'm still surprised I haven't had any weird cravings. I eat a lot but nothing like pickles and mayonnaise, just regular foods. I eat a lot of sweets and fruit, I hope that says a lot about the kind of person you'll be. Well, mommy loves you and can't wait to meet you.

Week 33

I'm so tired. I can't breathe, I can't walk. my whole body is swollen my eyes are almost shut. I can't thank God enough for allowing us to survive the car crash. I could've lost you, my mother, and my grandmother. But God kept all of us, he protected us and held you. I'm sorry that I risked the chance of losing you to run and save my mom, but I would hope one day you'll love me that much too. I don't know what I would've done or felt. But I just can't thank God enough.

I will die for you
without question, without second guessing
I will put my life in danger for you, on purpose
don’t worry I planned for this
I knew that in order to have you, there was this possibility carried with responsibility
but I need you in my life
for the little time I’ve known you, you've changed me
this is the purest form of physically expressing love
so I’ll do that for you
I don't think God would mind that I love you that much
it’s because of him that I even have you
every night I’ve read to you, sang to you, danced with you, stayed up late with you
so, when the time comes and you’re fully sprouted, and ready to leave what you've known as home
I pray I’ll be there to hold you, to kiss you, to protect you, for as long as I live
but if God has a different plan for us
just know there’s nothing and no one in this world I’ve loved more than you

Week 34

Well it's time to meet you. A little too soon but mommy has preeclampsia, which explains all the symptoms I've been having. You on the other hand are healthy and strong. The sound of your heartbeat soothes me. Every time you move and kick, I imagine you in my arms. I hope to see you in a couple hours

Week 34, day 4

After a long 72 hours of trying to dilate, breathe, contractions, mag in my veins, blood pressure skyrocketing, a fever hotter than the Sahara, a catheter in my urethra, a forced water breakage. They finally called for a failed induction. Mommy is so tired, I'm in so much pain. I just want you here. The doctors say with me having preeclampsia a c-section is supposed to happen but it's a risk for me, but I would take that risk over and over if it meant you would be healthy. You are my life, I have done what I wanted to do in this world which was to have you and love you. I will give my life with no hesitation if it means I can save you. In about 1 hour I pray I'll be meeting you. I love you.

April 18th 2019

Anyone can plant a seed in the ground

But can you get that seed to grow into the tree it's meant to be

Do you have the patience to wait, water it, cater to it,

Speak to it, love it, daily in order for it to sprout

In order for it to be all it can be

Tall and mighty

Vibrant

And here

as I bared life, I was broken
many nights went unslept as I let my reality take over my emotions
I am the one to blame
after all, I chose you
but I chose the old you
two powerful words removed the good in you
many days I tried to teach you love
I tried to show you a different definition
than the one you learned in your early years
but as I bared life
you tried your best to break me
you tried to convince me I was crazy
overlooking the signs thinking it would pass
when I came to you with the news, I was mortified at how you handled it
how you handled me
vulnerable, I couldn't help but feel helpless
those sweet eyes I loved so much turned into a hollow blackness
the words you chose had no remorse
and the proposition you presented was in no way your decision
be fruitful and multiply is the word we were given
I will not cheat this life out of living
fast forward
those sweet eyes replicated into this ray of sunshine I birthed
everyday I'm reminded of the man I fell in love with

as we both prepare
for the arrival of our child
we held the same joy in our hearts
but only I experienced joy and pain
I'm jealous of you because you're not alone
as you prepare to take a shower you hand your child off to
their father while I make room for mine to come in with me
this is your time to unwind, meditate, breathe, cry while I'm still
multitasking, entertaining, mothering, and worrying
I'm jealous of you because you have support
you weren't told to do it by yourself
you weren't left
in a chapter of my life I've looked forward to since a little girl
I've never been more disappointed in myself for choosing the
wrong person

the sun lightens my room before it arises outside
I wake up to tiny arms holding tight to my neck, a
palm placed gently on my cheek
the soft giggle I hear is far more soothing than
chirping birds
but it's nice to hear in the background
seven months ago I wouldn't label me a morning
person but now in the mornings you are my favorite
person
with my eyes still dilating I change your pampers and
hum what sounds like a lullaby but it's really a made-
up melody that represents how you make me feel
alive, loved, gentle, home, happy

In my dreams
decaf coffee and cream
sanford and son on the screen
sunlight spilling through the seams
lovingly rubbing the gift you planted in me
some time ago you kneeled down asking my hand in marriage
a sight I thought only my dreams would ever carry
I lie here while the man of my reality rubs my pregnant belly
he's protective of our treasure already, he sleeps with his arms wrapped
around your temporary home
I feel the growth in your bones, and the love in your veins
you are loved before sight

reality
ginger and warm peppermint tea
replaying old videos I've captured of my family
no light coming through the windows,
I'd rather sit in what's familiar
darkness
gently rubbing the gift I was surprisingly given
some time ago I imagined this chapter differently
a dream prayed to see with awaken eyes
I lie here with my whole heart in my belly
apologizing already, protective already, I sleep with my arms wrapped
around your home
I feel the strength of your kicks when I cry, and the love it represents
I am not alone
we love each other before sight

it's a shame that's how it always goes, from the concrete I rose.
from the tainted buildings and dirt roads.
from poverty and adversity I rose.
from a split family and hand-me-down clothes.
from the soil of mother earth I grow.
from the burns and scars I've beautified to unapologetically show.
from the graves of my past I rose.

Sickness and pain
Forced to deal with alone
Cruelty
Nothing but cruel to me
Words exchanged still haunting
Neither one of us ready but only one of us is willing to grow
Really neither of us really knows how to love or where to start
I lose myself in the trees
Too often I lose myself
Too often I forget I have to be strong not only for me
But for her growing inside of me
Sprouting like angry weeds, she's growing every week
We're growing apart at a time I really need you
I really need you
Just like you I've never done this

I've done a lot on my own this won't be the first
you're not the first person to choose me and use me I've been through much worse
I have humbled hearts more damaged than yours
I've listened to you make life plans that never seemed to include me
you never flinch at the thought of losing me
you've never considered the possibility of falling for a woman like me
you're too use to falling in hoes, I mean holes
too deep to climb out of
you're too use to temporary and counterfeit

I have decided that the image of me you have drawn out to your liking

Is not the image I shall bear the weight of any longer

You cannot define a spirit that you didn't take the time to understand

God told me that I'm covered with the sun and the moon

It is holy ground under these feet

I am the result of God's love and mercy

I have someone to teach now
And I can't teach what I haven't been practicing
So I'm starting now, and I'm starting with you
I do not give you permission to bring me to down anymore
I do not give you permission to use me
I do not give you permission to take my smile
I do not give you permission to belittle me
I do not give you permission to judge me
I do not give you permission to blame me
I do not give you permission to tear down my dreams
I do not give you permission to bring toxic energies
I do not give you permission to cause an unbalance in my chakras
I do not give you permission to leave your burdens with me
I do not give you permission to beat me with your own self hate
I do not give you permission to project your fears onto me
I do not give you permission to expect what you aren't willing to give
I do not give you permission to be inconsistent
I do not give you permission to blame your past for your actions
I do not give you permission to devalue me
I do not give you access to me
the moon is beneath me feet, I brought light into your world
you keep burning curtains trying to ignore the fact that I give you life
this crown made of twelve stars, how miraculous on this 12th month
I've realized my worth and is who is worthy

Woman

a dagger to my pride with every clinical visit
every positive test contradicted every lie
why is it so hard for it to just be you and I
what is so bad about the possibility of just you and I
you never cared for me
you never thought how your actions could affect me
giving into your flesh for a few minutes of pleasure
at the cost of my expense
and my healthiness
how dare you
how fucking dare you
and in such dependency to do so
you don't even know why you did it
over and over
you don't even know the history of the flesh you opened up
yet you so faithfully welcomed yourself
not a care for me or your unborn
I've never met anyone quite like you
that's for sure
and far, from a compliment

I have imagined plenty of times
I have wondered
times when everything becomes unbearable, I have questioned if
this is the way out
people have pushed me
situations have broken me
to a sharp point on the edge
I often wonder what's wrong with me
why do I think these things
what good will that do
It'll hurt you, how you hurt me
to remember your last words flow through my ears before my last
breath
I want you to feel guilty
maybe then you'll understand the power of words, the power of
humility and respect
but I'm worth more than having to prove
or play the game of getting back
my God can handle you better than I can

I stand in all shades brown.
I fight with the colored.
I fight for the murdered. In this shade will I be confident for I know my beauty is flawless.
I stand beside my colored man, tall and proud, with a love profound understanding of hurt and fire burning inside for freedom. I will stand in the fight next to women like me, next to women unlike me, unlikely to be friended because of the stereotypes placed upon me. I will stand.

when the world is on your shoulders the beings who were made from
your rib
stand for you
when men take your voice and your power, we remind you of who you
are, we remind you of your roots, we remind you of dignity
but who shows up for us
who reminds us of our importance, of our position, of our beauty
when the world belittles us, shames us, abuses us, steals from us,
manipulates us, silences us
who protects us when we are sexualized from the day we are born, up to
adulthood
who stands for us when we need it
we were made from your rib, we are front line in your war
we carry your burdens on our backs while you stand on a pedestal with
what society deems an acceptable partner
we hold the same features in our flesh but are labeled as everything
except beautiful
we are good enough in your eyes to lay down beside, to make babies, to
lust over but not worthy enough to commit and stay and build and love
and grow
angry? you damn right. bitter? you damn right.
tired? without a doubt. and don't forget sick.
for decades we have cried out and begged to our brothers for the same
energy we give
for the same instant reflex when society is standing on your necks
for the same unconditional love and forgiveness.
will we ever be enough to fight for? will we ever be enough to protect?

I say good morning to the smell of burnt hair, smoke fumes from the hot
comb, giggles and slow jams. Tip toeing into the kitchen that she
improvised into a salon
she's so interesting to look at when she's focused

conjuring up a plan of how I'm gonna run and grab hold to one of
her legs without her client noticing.
Potatoes, eggs, and sausage on the table waiting for me and my
brothers. How'd she manage to cook for us and then tend to
others?
I swear she can do anything.
She's a jack of all trades, I swear she does everything. I remember
the yellow home we use to live in, worn down and roach infested.
Paint chipping, squeaky wooden floors, no heat, just syrup
sandwiches to eat. I remember Tom and Jerry, honeycombs without
a bowl, milk going on 2 weeks old.
I remember cans of spaghetti-o's, juice cups. remember late nights
at the shop waiting for you to get off. A couple late nights at the
community center. I remember guy after guy, trying to find the
right one who could love the whole package of you and us. Being a
single mother can be a bit much. I remember you wanting to cry
but refusing to in front of us. You're too tough for us. I wish I could
see you vulnerable for once. You're human too, stop being
superwoman for once. I remember your belly with my brother
inside, so anxious to meet him.
I remember just about everyone you gave your heart to. I
remember how he left you. I remember the day he walked out. I
remember what that did to you, despite how beautifully you
covered it up. I remember how he hurt you, mentally and
physically. I remember what you said to me, thinking I'm too young
to know. I remember how you took us from nothing to everything. I
aspire to be something like you. Strong like you. Wise like you.
Fearless like you. Faith full like you. You find your answers in the
good book, I do too but most of the time I light nature on fire. I
can't stand to feel the lows of the world being woman and black, so
I get higher. I can't fathom another stab to this heart, so I like to get
higher

lately I've been spending time with me
digging deeper into myself, rejecting more and more invites
I've decided to stop neglecting me
I've decided that I don't mind losing others anymore
as long as I continue to hold onto myself, I'm whole
as long as each step is guided by God and each chapter is a lesson, I will
grow

I will surround myself with people who allow me to stand in my truth

I give myself permission to love those who want to love me, while still healing

I will give others love with no conditions as I would want to be given

I give myself permission to feel what I need to in each moment, fully

I will relish every second of this newfound love while it's here, and be not afraid of the future

I give myself permission to accept trial and error, to not be a perfect Mother but the best Mother I know how to be for mine

I will remember to ease up from being too hard on myself, too impatient in the process of my healing and remember things take time

I'm not a materialistic person
I don't have the normal gadgets the average person has in their home
but I have plants
some for home remedies, some to put my mind at ease
I have healing stones and an air purifier
some sage sticks and an antique metal iron
I'm not a fancy date person although I do enjoy dressing up
I'm horrible with small talk and uppity conversation
I feel out of place taking about stocks
but I can rant about energy conservation
my little ideas of how to save an endangered population
I'm not real big on gifts, more of the thought behind it
knowing that out of the twenty-four hours we're given
a portion of that was dedicated to me
I have valuable assets to offer
not things that can be thrown away
I don't want a just for the moment comfortability
I want a partnership and stability

when I think of the word strong
there flashes a glimpse of you
to watch you from a distance
conquer all the adversities that life threw
bearing life inside you for five months
never knowing the hurt that would later come
there's no words to describe the love that a mother and her unborn child share
but I'd imagine it's a warmth that no other soul could compare
what a feeling to know that there's an angel in heaven, who's only ever known you
I admire how you've dealt with pain
how like a butterfly you still glide through life gracefully
after all the injuries you've sustained
to me, you are the bravest lion in the den
you are the brightest daisy in the field, with the most petals too
you are the strongest tree in the forest
in my book of definitions, the epitome of strong is you

April 7th, 2016

I am valuable
worthy and loved

I am strong
wise and brave

I am the epitome of
love unconditional and plentiful

I am a pure soul
positive energy and good karma

I am the whistling wind
sunsets and shooting stars

I bring light into the darkness

I was not made to settle

listen, don't hand me no wooden nickels, she says
I'm a big cat not a kitten
you can't teach me no new tricks I'm an old dog, not no spring chicken
she says, I'm an old school grandma
this mulatto skinned, native blood in her veins
this woman, a bearer of two miscarriages with her backbone she carried us
this woman, strong and intelligent
godly, heaven sent
tough, thick skin
a proud and firm believer of what she's always known
forever standing in her first mind
change opens the door for the unknown
she says you ought to leave well enough alone
grey skies in her iris, she's seen many days like that
pain in the joints of her palms, working hands, picking up the slack of entitled men
you don't need a man she says
God made Eve for Adam, he's going to need you before you need him
you got a mind on you, before anything else you've got god's hands on you
you're invincible
life comes and goes, you've got a time cap on you
love comes and goes, just keep loving what's in front of you
she says, she wishes her mother where still here today
I've never told her, but I thank her for my mother everyday
the gentlest love ever shown
the most delicate souls I've ever known
the two responsible for this woman, and this growth

I'm often dismissed
Tugging away from becoming emotionless
Though it seems I'm always left with a nothingness
No one really knows me for real
Fading into oblivion
I'll be forgotten soon
I'm something like a closed open book
I wear my heart on my sleeves
And my frustrations on my shoulders
But I'm guarded
I don't show too much affection
I keep my feelings inside
But when I explode, I'll leave you dumbfound
I'm not very talkative
I've never had more than a handful of friends
But people always refer to me as their best friend
I guess people need listeners more than motivators
No one really thinks I have those days
No one really makes sure I don't have those days

Just think of how embarrassing it will be
When you're asked about the memories you have when she
was no bigger than two adult sized palms put together
What stories will you have to tell that will light up her eyes,
make her giggle and think one day I will know that feeling
What memories do you have other than my pleading and
begging for you to be there, for you to be present,
physically and emotionally
What memories other than pictures of me bonding and
showering my love onto her
Just think of how embarrassing it will be
When you're finally ready to be there and she doesn't know
you nor does she want to get to
And you will regret all those times I begged and pleaded
and the day I stopped
because I realized I'm all she ever needed

go ahead
ignore me I'm used to it
call me annoying
call me every name except the one that I was given
I'm used to it
get in my face
scream while I'm calm
disrespect me, curse me, put me down as a woman, as a mother
hurt me
go ahead
kick me while I'm down, while I'm sick, while I'm lost
keep kicking me until I'm lifeless
like I said I'm used to it
don't worry I'll pull through like I'm used to doing
I can see that karma has never visited you
you don't know of her capabilities
I see no one has ever told you about the repercussions of hurting
God's children
but I'm sure you'll find out, I'm certain
so go ahead continue to treat me how you've been
and I will continue to smile
I will continue to genuinely wish you a wonderful day
to humbly pray for your wellbeing
and continue to withhold speaking ill of you
publicly and in front of our seed
despite what you may say about me

September 19, 2019

I have a five-month-old, who is the light of my life
who so far has only met her father once, for seventy-two hours
I have a five-month-old, who thinks life is just me and her, the voice of me, the scent of me, the care and protection of me is all she thinks she's supposed to have
I have a five-month-old that I want to protect
who doesn't know that her mommy is broken but I guess that's a good thing
I have a five-month-old, who is happy just with the sight of me
but who deserves more
I have a five-month-old, who has a possible sibling
one that isn't growing inside of me
that I didn't hear about from her father

I don't know if I can take much more

I haven't been myself. Praying has gotten difficult. I've been thinking less, feeling more. When flashes of my reality catch me off guard, I've gotten used to the sudden drops in my core. Lately my heart stops when I spot a couple with their child happy... and together. Thinking why couldn't that be us, why couldn't she have that, why didn't he want that, why didn't I deserve that. Lately I've been praying for answers. Like, why should I want you here, why do I flood you with pictures and call you to hear her mumble when deep down you wish I... am not going to say it. Why should I let you in on the moments so special to me, knowing you'll only burn them with your negativity. Planting my face in his word I've been asking God for answers, but I've been afraid. I keep you in close proximity for the sake of her and my sanity, but I haven't been sane for some time. I haven't been myself, I've been wishing I could rewind.

Lately, I've been ashamed and fearful. That if I do what I know I need to, she'll punish me for your absence, she'll punish me for robbing her of a relationship. But, it's your decision to stay. I want you to be there in every way. But I want you to respect us and get out of your own selfish ways. I want you to be what she needs. But I won't allow you to mistreat me, not after all I've put up with, not after staring so close to death to bring our creation into this life. If you decide to walk away, that is your decision. I won't make it my concern. You have every right to stay.

Lately, I've been down.
Because now she's not the only one. Now she'll have to share you like I did. Now she'll have to compete like I did. How selfish of you to rob her, to rob us... of you.
Do you think that little of us? Do you think I'm that strong to carry your weight too? As if a mother's job isn't hard enough. You expect me to be a father too?

So that you can focus on being "that" father, to number two. How dare you.
Do we mean nothing to you?

Lately I've been lost.
I have two masks I carry throughout the day. One I wear in front of her and one for myself when I look in the mirror. Too ashamed, too scared to see what these scars look like.
Lately I've been pretending they don't exist. But I feel them, every day. How selfish of you to repeat the cycle with me, but break it for what's convenient... for what's familiar.

What good is having history if it's only a series of multiple sufferings.

Lord
I've learned my lesson
I understand what you were doing in my relationships
I understand why you let people leave me
I understand why you let them hurt me
I've learned my priorities are you, my child and myself
You tried to teach me my worth, but I didn't see it until now
I've learned someone should add to me not take way or fill in
This pain I feel today is unlike any other
I get it now
I shouldn't be chasing anyone but you, because whatever you have for me is mine
So thank you for making them flee
Thank you for putting me in solitude forcefully
Because I wouldn't have seen things on my own
I've learned that I can still be a blessing to people without giving everyone my heart
My heart has been empty for some time, but I still hand out its residue
I've always been left feeling like I'm not enough
Thinking I'm not woman enough or worthy to be loved
I've learned that your love is the only love worth fighting for, screaming for, chasing
Your love has been the only love returned to me
This world has never loved me
But I've learned my lessons so please don't send anyone else to hurt me
No more lessons, no more pain, no more signs
I get it Lord
I've realized what I've done

pain has always hidden in my shadows
I carry weight in my spirit
unwelcomed but yet the only thing constant I've experienced
my tear ducts are blocked from forcibly withholding built up emotions

What makes me worthy?

A certain tone in my skin or the limit of things I'm willing to put up with

Or maybe perfection on the outside not too concerning of what's rotting on the inside

Maybe it's what I can provide or what I'm willing to hide from you not so much what I will sacrifice

What makes me worthy?

I've never felt worth it

Worth the chase, worth the time, worth a sacrifice

I'm hurt that you thought so little of us,
to resort back to the past when the future held
so much weight

mourning bones
grieving spirit
pressure subsiding as the walls come down
do you see me?
now?
is this what you were waiting for?
is this what you were pressuring me to see?
what's the point in hiding?
you say, what's the point in hiding these scars?
I say, because no one has had the patience to let them heal first
they see me glow from the outside and want in right away
weary soul
weak flesh
I give in to him, my weakness
only to hurt again as the sun rises
only to lust again when our history deprives us
of being able to really work on us
only to be told I'm not it
only to be shown he's not fit
for me because I have a love only someone like me
can accept
do you see me now?
hmm?
how I've been here the whole time you were searching for love
with my heart on my shoulders I know you had to see it, love
did you see it? my love?
bright and beating for you
I opened up like you asked me to
I never asked you why you wanted to see what the past can do
insecurities wrapped around me connected like veins
submissive, my wrists in chains
on my knees praying for God to reign, on me
allergic to sun, scared of the light and mirrors

forgetting why I ever started a task or
why I even bothered waking up
do you see me now?
not her, but the woman I am
standing in front of you Godly
and brighter than the sun with a love for you
with no conditions or ultimatums
I want to love you
as long as you see me

my offspring
the result of light and darkness
but she blinds the world with her light
an aura bleeding yellow with a pinch of orange
she is the sun that sits in Aries
eyes full and angelic
she makes the stars in the night sky jealous
she is the moon full of Libras
she stares into my heart because only she knows how it truly sounds
when anxious, when sad, when panicking, when mellow
she stares into my heart like she knows
what I-
what he did
she stares into my heart like she already knows
she is the result of love, and loss
but she has never wandered
the first arms to ever hold her dripped tears infused with the purest love
my offspring
is the result of strength, faith, and favor

I love you E'lani

Keep up with the author:

Twitter and Personal Instagram: @selflessdiamond
Instagram: @wordsbydiamond

Made in the USA
Columbia, SC
05 November 2020